A Leader's Guide
to

We Can
Get Along

A Child's Book
of Choices

by
Lauren Murphy Payne, M.S.W., and
Claudia Rohling, M.S.W.

Illustrations by Claudia Rohling, M.S.W.

free spirit
PUBLiSHiNG®

Works
for kids®

Acknowledgments

We would like to acknowledge our publisher, Judy Galbraith, and our editor, Pamela Espeland, for their dedication to the well-being of children and their continued faith in our abilities.

The "25 Healthy Ways to Express Anger" Home Handout on page 32 is reprinted from *A Leader's Guide to Just Because I Am: A Child's Book of Affirmation* by Lauren Murphy Payne and Claudia Rohling. Minneapolis: Free Spirit Publishing, 1994. Used with permission.

Some of the information and suggestions in the "Celebrating Diversity" Home Handout on page 43 are adapted from *Respecting Our Differences: A Guide to Getting Along in a Changing World* by Lynn Duvall. Minneapolis: Free Spirit Publishing, 1994. Used with permission.

Book design and production by Rodney J. Gräu

10 9 8 7 6
Printed in the United States of America

Free Spirit Publishing Inc.
217 Fifth Avenue North, Suite 200
Minneapolis, MN 55401-1299
(612) 338-2068
help4kids@freespirit.com
www.freespirit.com

The following are registered trademarks of Free Spirit Publishing Inc.:

FREE SPIRIT®
FREE SPIRIT PUBLISHING®
THE FREE SPIRITED CLASSROOM®
SELF-HELP FOR KIDS®
SELF-HELP FOR TEENS®
WORKS FOR KIDS®
HOW RUDE!™
LEARNING TO GET ALONG™
LAUGH & LEARN™

Contents

List of Reproducible Pages

Introduction

Conflict is a normal part of life for all of us. In any relationship, we will experience conflict at some point or another. Children need to be taught how to deal effectively with conflict, not how to avoid it. They need to be taught that they have the power to choose their words and actions—and the consequences that follow. When children recognize that their words and actions have consequences, they begin to learn responsibility.

When used together with our children's book, *We Can Get Along: A Child's Book of Choices*, this Leader's Guide is a complete course in positive conflict resolution for young children. It is based on the core beliefs that:

- Conflict is a normal part of life that we need to deal with effectively.
- Children can learn to deal with conflict effectively by learning to recognize their own reactions to conflict and by learning to identify their feelings.
- Children can learn that they are responsible for things they say and do. They can learn to distinguish effective anger behaviors from those that escalate conflict.
- Children can learn to shift their focus from "How can *I* get what *I* want?" to "How can we *both* get what we need?"
- Children need to know that hitting is never okay.
- Children need to be empowered to remove themselves from hurtful situations.
- Children need to be taught the inherent value of all individuals, without regard to their differences or similarities.
- Children can be taught to validate the opinions of others and learn from them.

How to Use This Book

A Leader's Guide to We Can Get Along has been designed to be used in almost any setting where young children happen to be: kindergarten, early elementary school, preschool, day care, home, church or temple school, counseling group, and so on. The activities make full use of children's natural curiosity and creativity. Through reading, listening, questioning, creating, laughing, and loving, children learn that they are capable of getting along with others, making good choices, and resolving conflicts peacefully.

Before beginning the lessons, please read the children's book. Think about the words and what they mean to you. Look at the pictures and, if you like, invent stories to go along with each one. You will be sharing the words and pictures with the children in your group. You may want to ask the children to invent stories to go along with the pictures, and it will help to get them started if you are prepared with a few examples to share.

On page 3, you'll find a letter to parents and caregivers announcing and introducing "We Can Get Along." If you are presenting this course in a school or group setting, you'll want to make photocopies of this letter to send home with the children in your group.

On page 4, you'll find a second letter you may want to complete and use when sending program materials home with the children.

The children's book is divided into two-page sections that emphasize specific concepts in choice making, conflict resolution, and feelings identification. This Leader's Guide is divided into lessons that correspond to the children's book sections. Each lesson has four parts:

- an opening statement about the concept(s) being presented,
- a series of goals that describe the main ideas you will be communicating and what you hope to achieve,
- one or more activities to do with the children, and
- suggestions for follow-up that extend and/or reinforce the concepts taught in the lesson.

Many lessons also include one or more Home Handouts for you to photocopy and send home to parents.

The activities offer a variety of ways to teach the concepts and achieve the goals identified for each lesson. They are meant to be completely flexible. You may expand on them, adapt them, even eliminate some. Do whatever works best with the children in your group, depending on their interests and attention spans.

The suggestions for follow-up encourage the children to reflect on what they have learned in the lesson and how it applies to their lives. You may do these in the classroom right after the lesson, or wait until the following day or a later date. Again, it all depends on what works best with your group.

Please keep in mind that in doing the activities and follow-ups, your goal is not to control or define the children's behavior. There is no "right" way to learn how to get along with others. There are no "right" answers to the questions, no "right" approaches to the activities.

Allow children to access their own best ways of learning. Here are two suggestions that will help you to do this:

- Try to limit your input into the mechanics of doing the activities. Some children will color outside the lines, give silly-sounding answers to questions, or draw things that seem to have no relation to what they "should be" drawing. After all, they are children!
- Remind yourself often that all children have strengths. Some children's strengths may not be immediately evident. It's up to you to find something positive in *every* child in your group. Focus on strengths, and minimize the attention you give to behaviors that you would like to see less of.

We encourage you to use your own instincts, creativity, and imagination when presenting this course in conflict resolution. Our ideas may spark your ideas, and our lessons might be jumping-off points for wonderful learning experiences you invent.

Finally, *have fun*. If you communicate to the children that you are enjoying these lessons, they will enjoy them, too. What could be more fun and rewarding than learning how to get along with others?

Lauren Murphy Payne
Claudia Rohling

Dear Parent/Caregiver,

I'm writing to tell you about an exciting new course that the children and I will be starting very soon. It's called "We Can Get Along," and it teaches young children to resolve conflicts peacefully and effectively.

Conflict is a normal part of life for all of us. In any relationship, we will experience conflict at some point or another. Children need help learning how to get along with others, even during times of conflict. They need to know that they have the power to make good choices. "We Can Get Along" presents these concepts in ways young children can relate to and understand.

The course has fifteen lessons. The lessons are based on the picture book titled *We Can Get Along: A Child's Book of Choices*. The picture book uses simple statements and colorful illustrations to communicate important messages about conflict resolution and choice making. The lessons include questions and activities that reinforce these messages in a way that's fun for everyone. The emphasis throughout is on kindness, respect, tolerance, and responsibility.

During the course, you'll receive several Home Handouts related to the lessons. These handouts will keep you in touch with the ideas we're exploring in "We Can Get Along." If you want, you can use them to reinforce the lessons at home.

We will begin the course on_____ (date).
If you have any questions or comments at this time or any time during the course, please don't hesitate to contact me.

Yours sincerely,

_____

Telephone: _____

Dear Parent/Caregiver,

Attached are some materials from "We Can Get Along," the conflict resolution course in which your child is participating. I'm sending you these materials because:

If you have any questions about these materials or about "We Can Get Along," please be sure to contact me.

Yours sincerely,

_____

Telephone: _____

LESSON ONE
I Know Lots of People

Children need to understand that not everyone they meet will always be friendly, and that even friends don't always get along. They need to know that conflict is a normal part of many relationships.

GOALS

1. To make children aware of the many people they encounter and interact with in their daily lives.
2. To introduce the idea that conflict is normal.
3. To begin identifying ways in which people do and don't get along.

ACTIVITY

People We Know

Materials needed:

- Blank newsprint, butcher paper, or legal size paper, folded and cut into strings of 4 paper dolls (1 string for each child; older children can draw and cut out their own paper dolls)
- Safety scissors
- Crayons, markers, and/or colored pencils
- Small gummed stars in two different colors (such as red and blue), or other small gummed or adhesive stickers in two different colors
- Hole punch
- Several 6" lengths of colored yarn

Hand out the strings of paper dolls, or have older children make their own using folded paper and safety scissors (they may need help folding the paper correctly and tracing the shape to cut out). Then tell the children, "We all know lots of people. We see them at school, in the neighborhood, and on the playground. Think of four people you know who are not in your family. Decorate your paper dolls to look like those people."

When the children have finished drawing and coloring their paper dolls, give each child 8 small gummed stars (or stickers), 4 of each color. Say, "Sometimes we get along with the people we know, and sometimes we don't. Think of each paper doll person you made. If you usually get along with that person, stick a red star on the doll. If you sometimes *don't* get along with that person, stick a blue star on the doll. It's okay to put both colors of stars on the same doll."

When the children have finished applying their stars or stickers, use a hole punch and yarn to connect the strings of paper dolls. (Punch holes in the hands at the ends of each string, then tie the strings together with yarn to create one long string. The children can help you with this.) Display the final long string on a wall.

Call the children's attention to the string of paper dolls. Ask questions like:

- "What do you see when you look at the paper dolls?" (Lots of people.)
- "Do you see red stars? Do you see blue stars?" (They should see both.)
- "Do we *always* get along with the people we know? Are there times when we *don't* get along?"

Tell the children that *conflict*—not getting along— is a normal part of many relationships. Even friends don't always get along.

NOTE: You may want to keep the string of paper dolls on display for the duration of "We Can Get Along."

FOLLOW-UP

Have each child in turn identify one person in his or her string of paper dolls. (You may want to start with a volunteer.) Ask the child to tell about a time when they *did* get along. (*Example:* "This is my friend Marcus. We got along last week when we played in the park.") Then ask the child to tell about a time when they *didn't* get along. (*Example:* "Marcus wanted to play soccer, but I wanted to play basketball. I got mad because he wouldn't play what I wanted.")

As the children share their examples, continue to reinforce the point that conflict is normal. You might end by saying something like this:

"It sounds as if we all have times when we get along with people, and times when we don't. Conflict is a normal part of our everyday lives. This is true for everyone—you and your friends, your parents and teachers, and everyone else you know."

LESSON TWO
When We Get Along

For children to have healthy, positive relationships, they need to feel safe and able to trust other people. They need to be able to express their feelings, wants, and needs.

GOALS

1. To help children identify times and relationships that feel happy and safe for them.
2. To teach children how to express their feelings, wants, and needs by using simple "I messages."

ACTIVITIES

1. My Book of Being Happy and Feeling Safe

Materials needed:

- Blank books, one for each child (4–6 sheets of white 8 1/2" x 11" paper, stapled together with a copy of "My Book of Being Happy and Feeling Safe" on page 9 as the cover)
- Crayons, markers, and/or colored pencils

Invite the children to think about a time when they felt happy and safe. Ask questions like:

- "Where were you?"
- "Who were you with?"
- "What were you doing?"
- "Why were you happy?"
- "What felt safe to you?"

If the children need help, you might introduce and briefly discuss some of the items on the "25 Things That Friends Do" Home Handout on page 10.

Distribute the blank books and tell the children that they are going to create stories about a time when they felt happy and safe. Explain that they will tell their stories in pictures. Have them start by writing their name on the cover. (Very young children will need help with this; you may want to write their names on their books before handing them out.)

While the children are working, circulate among them, offering assistance and suggestions where needed. Encourage the children to think of this as their very own "picture book" of a wonderful time in their lives.

Afterward, allow time for the children to share their stories. Let them take their books home to show their parents or caregivers. If they want, they can ask their parents to write words to go along with their pictures.

2. Using "I Messages"

Introduce "I messages" by saying:

"Sometimes we don't feel happy and safe when we are with another person. We feel sad or angry or upset. We need to tell the other person how we feel. We need to do this without blaming the other person, because blaming can make a conflict even worse.

"When we say things like, 'YOU make me sad,' or 'YOU make me angry,' or 'YOU make me upset,' we are blaming the other person. That can make the other person feel like defending himself or herself. The other person might answer, 'No, YOU make ME feel that way.' Now you are having an argument!

"There's a better way to tell the other person how you feel. You can use an 'I message.' This is easy to do. Instead of starting off by saying 'You. . . ,' start off by saying 'I. . . .' Here are some examples:

- 'I feel sad when you don't want to play with me.'
- 'I feel angry when I can't share your toys.'
- 'I feel upset when you make faces at me.'

"You can also use 'I messages' to tell what you want or need from the other person. Like this:

- 'I want you to stop making faces at me.'
- 'I need you to share the ball or I can't play.' "

Ask the children to remember a time when they didn't get along with someone else. Have them invent some "I messages" they might use the next time that happens.

FOLLOW-UP

1. Talk more with the children about feeling happy and safe. Ask questions like:

- "Who are some people you trust?"
- "Who are some people you can talk to when you want to talk?"
- "Who helps you when you need help?"
- "What are some other things that make you feel happy and safe?"

2. Role play using "I messages" in different situations. Explain that other people can't know how we feel unless we tell them. They can't guess what we want and need.

3. Copy the Home Handout for this lesson, "25 Things That Friends Do," to send home to parents/caregivers. You might use the letter on page 4 to introduce the handout and suggest that parents discuss with their child some or all of the items on the list.

My Book of Being Happy and Feeling Safe

by

_____

NAME

25 THINGS THAT FRIENDS DO

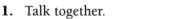

1. Talk together.

2. Laugh together.

3. Work together.

4. Play together.

5. Share quiet times.

6. Help each other.

7. Encourage each other.

8. Praise each other.

9. Stick up for each other.

10. Try to see each other's point of view.

11. Think about each other's wants and needs.

12. Think about how they want to be treated. Treat each other that way.

13. Use kind words.

14. Use gentle touches.

15. Treat each other with respect.

16. Share their feelings with each other.

17. Ask for what they need.

18. Listen to each other.

19. Solve problems together.

20. Compromise when they don't agree.

21. Understand that sometimes people feel angry, sad, or afraid.

22. Know that it's not okay to take out their anger, sadness, or fear on each other.

23. Keep their hands and feet to themselves when they feel angry.

24. Say "I'm sorry" when they say or do hurtful things.

25. Know that it's okay to sometimes disagree with each other.

LESSON THREE
When We Don't Get Along

Children need to recognize what they do and how they feel during times of conflict. This prepares them to learn peaceful and effective ways to resolve conflict.

GOALS

1. To help children identify words and actions that cause or escalate conflict.
2. To introduce the concept that we are all responsible for our own words and actions.

ACTIVITIES

1. Anger Chemistry

Materials needed:

- Clear glass bowl
- Box of baking soda
- Small bottle of vinegar
- Measuring cup
- Teaspoon or measuring spoon

Put the bowl, the baking soda, the bottle of vinegar, and the teaspoon on a table and gather the children around it. Pour a small amount of vinegar (about 1/2 cup) in the bowl.

Invite volunteers to tell about a time when they didn't get along with someone else. Ask:

- "What did the other person do or say?"
- "What did *you* do or say?"

For each example given, add a small amount of baking soda (1/4 teaspoon or so) to the bowl of vinegar. (Older children can do this themselves.) Explain that this is what happens when two people don't get along: One person (the baking soda) says or does something that causes the other person (the vinegar) to react with anger and fear (fizzing, bubbling).

NOTE: Eventually the vinegar and baking soda solution will become saturated and the chemical reaction won't occur. If you want to continue the experiment, rinse the bowl and start over.

2. Things That Friends Don't Do

Materials needed:

- Poster paper and easel (or tape the paper to a chalkboard or wall)
- Markers

Invite the children to brainstorm things that friends don't do and say—actions and words that lead to conflict or escalate conflict. Write down their responses on the poster paper. (If the children have difficulty getting started, give a few examples from the "25 Things That Friends Don't Do" Home Handout on page 13.) Have the children tell about times when other people did or said these things, and times when they did or said them. Relate their examples to the Anger Chemistry experiment of Activity #1. Every so often, ask:

- "If the other person (hits, kicks, teases, calls names, or some other example), who is responsible for causing the conflict or making it worse? Who is putting the baking soda in the vinegar?"
- "If you (hit, kick, tease, call names, or some other example), who is responsible for causing the conflict or making it worse? Who is putting the baking soda in the vinegar?"

Gently emphasize to the children that they are responsible for their own words and actions during times of conflict—and other times as well.

NOTE: Be sure to save the brainstormed list generated during this lesson. You will use it again in future lessons.

FOLLOW-UP

1. Say to the children, "We just talked about things we do and say that cause conflict or make it worse. Can you think of things we do and say that stop conflict from happening or make it better?" You might refer to the "25 Things That Friends Do" Home Handout from Lesson Two (page 10).

2. Ask the children, "When you feel angry or afraid, who can you talk to about your feelings? Who can you ask for help?" Encourage them to think of the people in their lives—parents/caregivers, teachers, friends, older siblings—as possible sources of comfort and help.

3. Copy the Home Handout for this lesson, "25 Things That Friends Don't Do," to send home to parents/caregivers. You might include a note to parents encouraging them to talk with their child about these behaviors. Parents might also compare "25 Things That Friends Don't Do" with "25 Things That Friends Do" from Lesson Two and talk with their child about the differences between these behaviors.

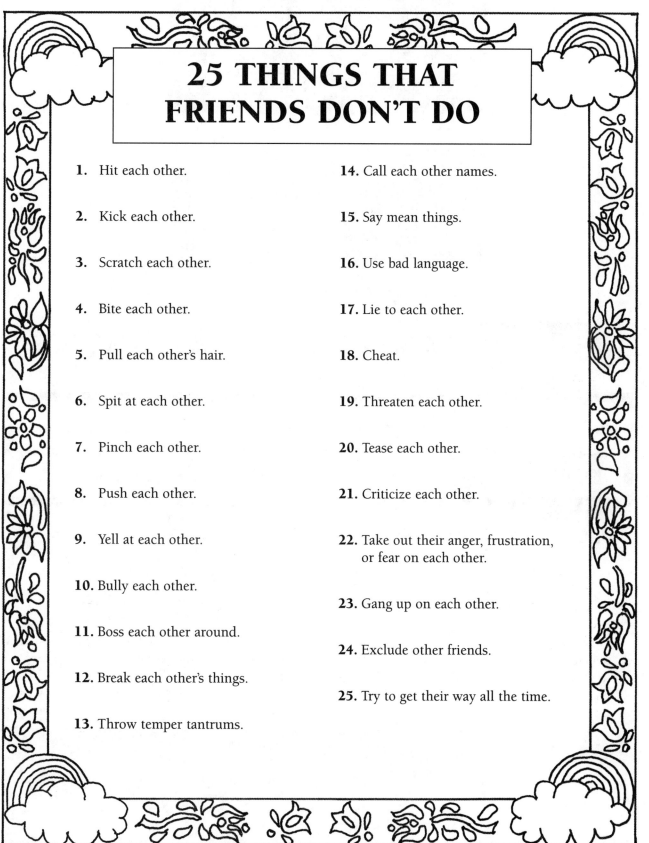

25 THINGS THAT FRIENDS DON'T DO

1. Hit each other.

2. Kick each other.

3. Scratch each other.

4. Bite each other.

5. Pull each other's hair.

6. Spit at each other.

7. Pinch each other.

8. Push each other.

9. Yell at each other.

10. Bully each other.

11. Boss each other around.

12. Break each other's things.

13. Throw temper tantrums.

14. Call each other names.

15. Say mean things.

16. Use bad language.

17. Lie to each other.

18. Cheat.

19. Threaten each other.

20. Tease each other.

21. Criticize each other.

22. Take out their anger, frustration, or fear on each other.

23. Gang up on each other.

24. Exclude other friends.

25. Try to get their way all the time.

LESSON FOUR
I Can Remember My Feelings

Children need to know that they have the power to choose their words and actions. They need to become more aware of their feelings and develop a "feelings vocabulary"—a set of words that describe various feelings.

GOALS

1. To teach children that they have choices regarding their words and actions.
2. To reinforce the concept introduced in Lesson Three that we are all responsible for our own words and actions.
3. To help children develop a "feelings vocabulary."
4. To encourage children to use their own feelings as guides when choosing their words and actions.

ACTIVITIES

1. The Faces We Wear

Materials needed:

- The "Things That Friends Don't Do" list that children brainstormed during Lesson Three
- Heavy round or oval paper plates
- Crayons, markers, and/or colored pencils
- Art supplies: Paints, glitter, confetti, yarn, ribbon, wrapping paper, pipe cleaners, etc.
- Glue sticks
- Yarn, ribbon, or string
- Safety scissors
- Hole punch

Introduce this activity by telling the children that they have the power to choose their words and actions. Review the "Things That Friends Don't Do" list the children brainstormed during Lesson Three. Or you might use selections from the "25 Things That Friends Don't Do" Home Handout from Lesson Three (page 13).

Ask the children to remember a time when they didn't act like a friend. Have them make the face they were "wearing" at that time. (Expect scowls, frowns, angry looks, sad looks, etc.) Next, have them create a paper-plate mask of the face. Start by helping them cut out holes for the eyes. After the children finish decorating their masks, punch holes in both sides and tie lengths of yarn, ribbon, or string in the holes so the children can wear their masks.

Group the children in pairs. Have them take turns wearing their masks and role playing the times when they didn't act like a friend. (Remind the children not to actually hit, push, or kick each other, even if that's what they originally did.) The child not wearing the mask should respond with an "I message." (*Example:* "I feel sad when you say mean things to me.")

Afterward, have the children put down their masks and role play positive ways they could have acted instead. If they need help, share some or all of the items on the "25 Things That Friends Do" Home Handout from Lesson Two (page 10). Partners should respond with "I messages." (*Example:* "I feel happy when you play with me.")

2. Naming Our Feelings

Tell the children, "There are many different words we can use to describe our feelings. The more words we know, the more clearly we can talk about our feelings. This helps other people to understand us better."

Read a selection of feelings words from the "50 Words That Describe Feelings" Home Handout on page 16. As you read each word, ask:

- "Who knows what this word means?"
- "Who can tell about a time when you felt this way?"

Give examples and invite the children to do the same:

- "I feel joyful when I take a walk on a beautiful day."
- "I feel calm when I pet my cat."
- "I feel fidgety when I have to sit still."

FOLLOW-UP

1. Talk with the children about the role plays. Ask:

- "How did you feel when you *didn't* act like a friend?"
- "How did you feel when you *did* act like a friend?"
- "How did you feel when your partner *didn't* act like a friend?"
- "How did you feel when your partner *did* act like a friend?"

Explain to the children that they can *choose* to act like a friend or not. Remind them that they are responsible for their own actions and words.

2. Make the connection between feelings and choices. You might say something like:

"We can remember our feelings after we have them. When you were younger, you probably learned not to go near a hot stove. Maybe you tried it once and got burned or almost got burned. That was a scary feeling! You remember that feeling, and it helps you *choose* to stay away from the stove. You *stop* before you get too close.

"You can also remember how it felt when someone you know didn't act like a friend. You can remember feeling sad, angry, or afraid. You can *stop* before you do or say something that might hurt someone else. You can *choose* to be a friend."

3. Copy the Home Handouts for this lesson, "50 Words That Describe Feelings" and "Helping Children to Say What They Mean," to send home to parents/caregivers. You might include a note encouraging parents to help their child build a "feelings vocabulary." One way to do this is by being straightforward about their own feelings!

50 WORDS THAT DESCRIBE FEELINGS

Words that build a "feelings vocabulary". . .
for kids and parents to practice together

happy	surprised	fearful
excited	startled	embarrassed
eager	afraid	guilty
joyful	shocked	self-conscious
"on top of the world"	terrified	ashamed
sad	shy	safe
"down"	bashful	secure
gloomy	helpless	confident
miserable	lonely	hopeful
tearful	unsure	trusting
fidgety	confused	irritated
anxious	puzzled	mad
tense	mixed-up	angry
worried	distracted	upset
restless	tired	furious
	calm	
	content	
	satisfied	
	proud	
	relaxed	

HELPING CHILDREN TO SAY WHAT THEY MEAN

In addition to helping children build a "feelings vocabulary" so they can express their feelings, we adults need to help them say what they really mean.

Children often repeat what they have heard. (That's why they sometimes say strange or shocking things!) They don't always know what they are saying or realize the impact their words may have. We can offer alternatives to aggressive, blaming, and inaccurate language. When we do this, we give children powerful tools for building healthy relationships and resolving conflicts peacefully and effectively.

Talk with your child about these examples. Add others from your own experience with your child.

When your child says. . .	*Your child probably means. . .*
• "I hate you!" • "You're stupid!"	• "I am angry with you!" • "I don't agree with what you are saying/doing."
• "You don't care about me!" • "Get away from me!" • "You're so mean to me!"	• "I am really sad." • "I need to be alone." • "That really hurts me."

LESSON FIVE
My Words and Actions Belong to Me

Children need to understand that they "own" their words and actions. They are responsible for what they choose to say and do. They can learn to consider their words and behaviors before they speak and act.

GOALS

1. To reinforce the concept introduced in Lesson Three that we are all responsible for our own words and actions.
2. To give children a sense of ownership of their words and actions.
3. To teach children to stop and think before speaking or acting, especially in conflict situations.

ACTIVITIES

1. My Words and Actions Collection

Materials needed:

- Small paper sacks (lunch-bag size)
- An assortment of small soft and hard objects (cotton balls, fabric scraps, twigs, stones, etc.) in a large, shallow box or tray
- Crayons, colored pencils, and/or markers

Begin this activity by reading these words from the children's book, *We Can Get Along:*

**"I am in charge of my words and actions. . .
They belong to me."**

Then ask, "Who can tell me what that means?" Allow time for discussion. Offer a few examples like the following, using the names of the children in your group:

- "If John tells Jessica, 'I'm glad you're my friend,' who is saying the words? Who 'owns' the words?"
- "If Keesha tells Sam, 'I don't want to play with you,' who is saying the words? Who 'owns' the words?"
- "If Jacob helps Alex put his toys away, who is doing the helping? Who 'owns' that action?"
- "If Kim pushes Blake on the playground, who is doing the pushing? Who 'owns' that push?"

Give each child a small paper sack. Explain that the children will use it to hold a "words and actions collection." Have them write their names on their bags. (For very young children, you might want to label the bags before you hand them out.)

Direct the children's attention to the box or tray of small objects. Say something like:

"These things stand for words and actions. The soft ones stand for things that friends say and do. The hard ones stand for things that friends don't say and do." At this point, you might offer a few examples from the "25 Things That Friends Do" Home Handout from Lesson Two (page 10) and the "25 Things That Friends Don't Do" Home Handout from Lesson Three (page 13). Afterward, say something like:

"Think about things you have said and done. Then choose a few items to put in your bag."

Allow a few minutes for the children to select objects for their bags. Have the children keep their bags with them for the rest of this lesson. Let them take their "collections" home to show their parents or caregivers.

2. The "Stop and Think" Necklace

Materials needed:

- Copies of the "Stop/Think" handout on page 20 (best if copied on heavy paper)

- Safety scissors
- Crayons, colored pencils, and/or markers
- Hole punch
- Tape
- Colorful ribbons or long shoelaces

Introduce this activity by saying:

"Did you ever say something you wish you hadn't said? Did you ever do something you wish you hadn't done? This happens to everyone, especially during times of conflict. But we can learn to *stop* and *think* before we say or do anything."

Give each child a copy of the "Stop/Think" handout. Read the words aloud or ask a volunteer to read them. Let the children color the stop sign and "thought bubble." Cut them out along the solid line or invite the children to help you. Fold on the dotted line. (You may want to tape the edges together, at least along the top.) Punch two holes in the top corners (through both layers of paper). String lengths of colorful ribbon or shoelaces through the holes to make necklaces.

Tell the children, "You have the power to *stop* and *think* before you speak or act. This necklace will remind you to do that. If you don't want to wear the necklace, you can keep it in your pocket as a reminder."

NOTE: Save an example of the "Stop and Think" necklace. You will refer to it again in future lessons.

FOLLOW-UP

1. Remind the children to take their "collections" home. You might also send a note home to parents/caregivers explaining the activity. Tell them that the soft objects relate to "25 Things That Friends Do," the hard objects relate to "25 Things That Friends Don't Do," and the "collection" is another way to teach children that they are responsible for their words and actions.

2. Suggest that the children practice *stopping* and *thinking* between now and the next time you meet.

1. Cut along the dark line →

2. Fold on the dotted line →

LESSON SIX
I Can Do My Part to Get Along

Children need to know that other people have wants and needs, too. In their relationships with others, they can learn to shift their focus from "How can *I* get what *I* want?" to "How can we *both* get what we need?"

GOALS

1. To introduce the concepts of negotiation and compromise as problem-solving techniques.
2. To help children identify the things they do that help to build relationships and resolve conflicts.

ACTIVITY

Partners Art

Materials needed:

- Large sheets of paper
- Crayons, colored pencils, and/or markers
- Paints

Group the children in pairs. Tell them that they are going to work together to draw and color pictures. Ask them to start by thinking about the picture they want to make. Ask questions like:

- "What do *you* want to draw?"
- "What do you think *your partner* wants to draw? How can you find out?" (By asking and then listening to what the other person says.)
- "How can you make sure that your picture is something you *both* want to draw?"
- "How can you make sure that your final picture is something you *both* like and feel proud of?"

Invite the children to brainstorm ideas. If they have difficulty getting started, offer a few examples like the following, using the names of the children in your group:

- "If Tiffany has an idea for a picture, she can tell Mandy, and Mandy can listen to Tiffany's idea."
- "Michael and Kate can think together about what colors they want to use."
- "Maybe Shannon can draw the outlines and Roy can color them in."
- "If Montel likes to draw trees, maybe he can do that part. If Ellie likes to draw houses, maybe she can do that part."

Give the children time to make their drawings. If a pair gets stuck or seems headed toward disagreement or conflict, tell them to *stop* and *think* before proceeding. Remind them that friends:

- work together
- help each other
- encourage each other
- listen to each other
- solve problems together, and
- compromise when they don't agree.

NOTE: These suggestions are all from the "25 Things That Friends Do" Home Handout from Lesson Two (page 10).

FOLLOW-UP

Have the children show their drawings to the group. Praise each drawing in turn. Invite the children to tell about how they worked together. Ask questions like:

- "How did you decide what to draw?"
- "How did you choose the colors?"
- "Was it easy or hard to work together? What made it easy? What made it hard?"
- "Did you have any disagreements along the way? How did you solve them?"
- "Were there any disagreements you couldn't solve? What did you do?"

When you have seen all of the drawings, you might say something like:

"There's something special about *all* of the drawings. If only *one* person had drawn each one, they just wouldn't be the same! You all did your part to get along and make your drawings, and I'm very proud of you."

LESSON SEVEN
I Know How I Like to Be Treated

One of the best ways to teach children kindness and respect is by our own example. We can create caring environments in our homes and classrooms, and we can model behaviors we want children to emulate. We can also encourage children to treat others with kindness and respect—and help them to understand that if *they* like to be treated this way, it stands to reason that *others* do, too.

GOALS

1. To help children articulate how they like to be treated, and to acknowledge that it feels good to be treated with kindness and respect.
2. To encourage children to perform small acts of kindness for others.

ACTIVITIES

1. An Especially Warm Welcome

As the children enter the room (or as you begin this lesson), go out of your way to welcome them with extra warmth and kindness. (If you're already someone who demonstrates your affection for the children in your group, you may have to go overboard!) Be sure to greet each child by name. Show by your words, actions, facial expressions, and body language how glad you are to see them and be with them today.

Try to say something special and unique to every child. (*Examples:* "Calvin, I notice that you're wearing your green shirt today. I really like that shirt!" "Jennifer, thanks for hanging your coat up so neatly. I appreciate that!" "Alicia, what a nice smile!" "I see you got a haircut, Denzel! It looks great!")

When all of the children have arrived, have them give each other extra special greetings.

2. The Act of Kindness Gift Certificate

Materials needed:

- Copies of the "Act of Kindness Gift Certificate" on page 25
- Business-size envelopes
- Pencils, crayons, colored pencils, and/or markers

Optional:

- Art supplies: Colorful stickers, glitter, ribbon, etc.
- Glue sticks

Begin by asking the children to tell about a time when someone did something nice for them. These can be simple, everyday incidents; perhaps a parent read a bedtime story, a sibling helped them tie their shoes, a friend shared a toy, or. . . . If they need help getting started, you might share an experience from your own life.

Encourage each child to give an example. Add brief, supportive comments along the way, such as, "That was really nice, wasn't it?" "What a great story! Thank you for telling us about it." "That person was very kind to you, wasn't he/she?" Afterward, ask the children, "How do you feel when someone treats you with kindness?" They probably will respond, "I feel good" or "I feel happy."

Say, "If you feel good/happy when someone does something kind for you, how do you think other people feel when you do something kind for them?" Explain that acts of kindness can be very powerful. They can spread good feelings all around.

Tell the children that today they will make gift certificates for people in their families. Their gift certificates will describe or illustrate acts of kindness they promise to do. Emphasize that these can be simple things—helping a parent set the table for dinner, offering to do a chore "just because," giving a hug, sharing a favorite toy, comforting a sibling who is feeling sad. You might spend a few moments brainstorming ideas with the children.

(Also make sure that they understand the concept of a gift certificate. If they don't, explain it to them.)

Give each child a copy of the "Act of Kindness Gift Certificate" handout and an envelope. Read the words aloud or ask a volunteer to read them. Have them decide who will receive their certificate and write that person's name on the "To" line. They should then write their own name on the "From" line. (Younger children will need help with this.) Have them complete their certificates by drawing or writing about the act of kindness they promise to do.

When the children have completed their gift certificates, have them fold them and put them in envelopes to take home. If time allows, they can decorate their envelopes.

FOLLOW-UP

1. Talk with the children about their gift certificates. Ask questions like:

- "What can be exciting about giving someone a gift certificate?"
- "When will you give your gift certificate to the person?"
- "When will you do your act of kindness?"
- "How does it feel to make a plan to do something nice for someone?"

2. Send a note home to parents/caregivers explaining the "Acts of Kindness Gift Certificate" activity. You might encourage them to respond by note or phone and tell you how the act of kindness was given and received.

ACT OF KINDNESS
GIFT CERTIFICATE

To: _____

From: _____

I promise to do this for you:

LESSON EIGHT
I Don't Like Mean Words

Children need to understand that words can hurt. They need to know that they have choices when other people say mean words to them—and when they feel like saying mean words to others.

GOALS

1. To help children understand that words have the power to hurt.
2. To brainstorm positive responses to hurtful words and remind children that they can choose not to use hurtful words.

ACTIVITIES

1. Sticks and Stones

Materials needed:

- Poster paper and easel (or tape the paper to a chalkboard or wall)
- Markers

Ask the children, "Have you ever heard the saying, 'Sticks and stones may break my bones, but names will never hurt me'?" Most children probably will have heard this saying. If some haven't, ask another child to explain it.

When you're sure that everyone understands it, ask, "Is it true that names don't hurt? What about bad names? What about mean words?" Ask the children to describe how they feel when someone calls them a bad name or says mean words to them. List their feelings on the poster paper. If the children need help naming their feelings, you might refer to the "50 Words That Describe Feelings" Home Handout from Lesson Four (page 16), which lists several negative feelings as well as positive ones.

Ask the children, "When someone says mean words to you, what can you do?" Help them to brainstorm alternatives, and list them on poster paper. Each suggestion should begin with "I can. . . ." Possibilities include:

- "I can walk away."
- "I can pretend not to hear."
- "I can tell an adult."

Encourage the children to suggest some "I messages" they might use in response to mean words. List them on poster paper, too. Examples:

- "I don't like it when you say that to me."
- "I feel sad when you call me names."
- "I want you to stop saying those words."

End by saying something like:

"Mean words can hurt our feelings, just like sticks and stones can hurt our bodies. You have choices about what to do when someone says mean words to you. And you can choose not to say mean words to other people."

Ask the children if anyone remembers the "Stop and Think" necklace they made in Lesson Five. Show them an example of the necklace. Remind them that they can *stop* and *think* before they say mean or hurtful things.

2. Mean Word Monster Basketball

Materials needed:

- Drawing paper
- Colored paper
- Crayons, colored pencils, and/or markers
- Masking tape
- Waste basket
- Small treats of some kind (gummy animals, M&Ms, animal crackers)

Tell the children that mean words are like monsters. Have them draw the meanest-looking monsters they can imagine. Then have them crumple their drawings into balls.

Stick two lines of masking tape to the floor, side-by-side horizontally. Position the waste basket some distance in front of the lines (the distance will depend on how far you think the children can easily throw their paper balls). Divide the group into two teams, and have the teams line up behind the masking-tape lines. Have the children take turns throwing their "monster balls" into the basket, and reward each successful throw with a small treat. (Children who miss can have another chance; this isn't a serious competition. Make sure that all children get to throw their "monster balls" into the basket; make sure that all children get a treat.) Afterward, talk with the children about how it felt to throw away their "mean word monsters."

FOLLOW-UP

Tell the children to practice what they have learned today—with their friends, in their group, in their families. Remind them that they now know some positive things to do when people say mean and hurtful words to them. Encourage them to *stop* and *think* before saying mean words to other people.

LESSON NINE
Hitting Is Never Okay

Children need to know that hitting is always unacceptable. They need to learn ways to express their anger that don't involve hurting others or getting physical with them.

GOALS

1. To teach children alternatives to releasing their anger by physically hurting or attempting to hurt others.
2. To emphasize and reinforce that hitting is never okay.
3. To encourage children to spread the message that hitting is never okay.

ACTIVITIES

1. Clay Ball

Materials needed:

• Enough modeling clay to form 3–4 large balls

Gather the children around a table with the clay. Have them work together to make large balls out of the clay. They should manipulate the clay enough that it becomes malleable and fairly soft.

Tell the children to remember a time when they were so angry that they wanted to hit someone. Have each child in turn throw a clay ball on the floor with all of his or her anger and might. The children should throw the balls as hard as they can. Tell them to pay attention to what happens to the clay when they throw it.

After everyone has had a chance to throw a clay ball, ask the children:

• "What happens to a clay ball when you throw it?" (It gets smashed.)

- "What happens to people when we get angry at them and take out our anger in physical ways?" (They can get hurt.)
- "Is it okay to throw a clay ball when you feel angry?" (Yes, this is an acceptable anger behavior—as long as you don't throw it *at* someone!)
- "Is it okay to hurt a person when you feel angry?" (No, this is never an acceptable anger behavior.)
- "If you are having a problem with another person, does pushing, kicking, or hitting make the problem better or worse? Why?" (Allow time for discussion.)

2. Healthy Ways to Express Anger

Materials needed:

- Poster paper and easel (or tape the paper to a chalkboard or wall)
- Markers

Say to the children:

"Sometimes we get so angry that our anger seems to fill us up. We need to let it out! If we don't *stop* and *think*, we might let out our anger by pushing, kicking, or hitting someone else. There are better ways to let out our anger—ways that don't hurt other people."

Invite volunteers to brainstorm healthy ways to express anger. List their ideas on the poster paper. If the children need help, you might introduce and briefly discuss some of the items on the "25 Healthy Ways to Express Anger" Home Handout on page 32.

3. The "Hitting Is Never Okay" Campaign

Materials needed:

- Blank newsprint, butcher paper, poster paper, or other large sheets of paper for posters and banners
- Balloons and string
- Crayons, colored pencils, and/or markers
- Art supplies: Glitter, confetti, yarn, ribbon, wrapping paper, pipe cleaners, colorful stickers, etc.

- An assortment of magazines with pictures
- Adhesive tape and glue sticks
- Safety scissors

Optional:

- Video camera and blank tape; cassette recorder and blank cassette

Work with the children to plan a "Hitting Is Never Okay" campaign for your classroom, preschool, day care, or wherever you are using "We Can Get Along." (Depending on how much you and the children want to do, you may decide to carry this campaign into more than one lesson, and you may want to involve more than one group or classroom.) Have the children work together to make and decorate posters, banners, collages, booklets, or whatever else they choose. They can blow up balloons, write "Hitting Is Never Okay" on them in markers, and display them in colorful bunches in the classroom, halls, or other public places. They can write and perform skits and songs for you to videotape and record. If you're at a school that has morning announcements, children can write "public service announcements" for broadcast. You might schedule the campaign to "premiere" at an open house or PTA meeting, and invite local media to attend. You can take this as far as you and the children want to go.

FOLLOW-UP

1. Talk with the children often about healthy ways to express anger. They cannot hear too often that physical violence is *never* acceptable.

2. Copy the Home Handout for this lesson, "25 Healthy Ways to Express Anger," to send home to parents/caregivers. You might use the letter on page 4 to introduce the handout and suggest that parents talk with their child about the items on the list. Take this opportunity to tell parents about the "Hitting Is Never Okay" campaign.

3. Most schools and many communities have anti-violence initiatives. You might see if your "Hitting Is Never Okay" campaign can be part of a broader local effort.

What to Do If a Child Says, "But Mommy/Daddy Hits Me"

As you talk with the children about alternatives to hurting others, and as you emphasize that "hitting is never okay," you may encounter this dilemma. Many parents believe that hitting and spanking are acceptable ways to discipline their children. Corporal punishment is legal in schools in many states (although it is our hope that you don't choose to use it with the children in your care).

What can you do? You can acknowledge that some parents/caregivers do, in fact, hit their children. Some parents/caregivers feel that hitting is an acceptable way to discipline children. Try not to get caught up in a discussion of this issue. Instead, draw the children's attention back to the main focus of this course: learning to get along with others at school, in the neighborhood, and on the playground. Then continue with one or more of the following statements:

- "Some people may feel that hitting is okay, but it is *not* okay in this classroom/group."
- "Hitting is *not* something that friends do to each other."
- "Remember that you are responsible for your own words and actions. You can *stop* and *think* before saying or doing anything to hurt someone else."
- "Remember how you like to be treated. You don't like it when someone hits you. Other people don't like it when you hit them. You can treat other people the way you like to be treated."
- "There are many healthy ways to express anger. Hitting is not one of them." (You might review the "25 Healthy Ways to Express Anger" Home Handout on page 32.)
- "You can't control what other people do. You can only control what *you* do. You can choose not to hit anyone in this classroom/group. If everyone makes that choice and sticks with it, there won't be any hitting here. Won't that be great?"

Not all parents/caregivers who hit their children believe that it's the right thing to do. Some are repeating behaviors they learned from their parents; some simply don't know how to use alternatives. During the course of your "Hitting Is Never Okay" campaign, or at some other point during "We Can Get Along," one or more parents might approach you and raise this issue, directly or indirectly. If this happens, try not to be judgmental or jump to conclusions. Instead, you might talk in general terms about how much we've all learned about parenting and child development in the past few decades. For example, you might mention that ideas about discipline and punishment are changing, and more parents are becoming aware of other techniques that work well, such as "time outs." If the parents seem interested, you might suggest that they read one or more books on parenting (for starters, see the list of books for adults in "Recommended Reading" on pages 55–56).

Depending on the situation and the rapport you have with the parents, you might refer them to Parents Anonymous. Founded in 1970, PA is a self-help organization with chapters in many cities and towns across the United States. It was originally begun by and for abusing parents, and some PA members are referred by the courts or child protection services, but many others are there because they need the support of other parents and they sincerely want to improve their parenting skills.

A PA group is a nonjudgmental, nonthreatening place to share thoughts and feelings freely, hear from other parents who have "been there," and brainstorm solutions to the stresses, tensions, and problems of parenting. Check your local telephone directory for the chapter nearest you, or contact the national organization:

Parents Anonymous, Inc.
675 W. Foothill Boulevard, Suite 220
Claremont, CA 91711
Telephone: (909) 621-6184
www.parentsanonymous.org

What to Do If You Suspect That a Child Is Being Abused

The regulations governing the reporting of child abuse differ from state to state. If you suspect that a child is being abused, contact your local Social Service or Child Welfare Department. You can also obtain information about what to do and how to report child abuse from your local Police Department or District Attorney's office.

If you are a teacher in a public school, consult *first* with your school principal to learn what the proper course of action is in your district.

Many states have specific guidelines identifying certain professionals as "mandatory reporters." This means that those professionals are required by law to report any suspected child abuse. Some states have provisions in their laws to protect the identity of those reporting child abuse. Check with your local agencies to determine your rights and responsibilities.

If a child reports abuse to you at any point during the course of "We Can Get Along," DO NOT attempt to further interview the child. Let the child speak about what is happening to him or her, and affirm to the child how difficult it must be to be in that situation. Offer suggestions within the context of the lesson on ways that the child might handle the situation. After the lesson, and with regard to the laws of your state or organization, act promptly in reporting the abuse.

Do not ask the child leading questions about what is happening to him or her. Leave that to professionals who have been specially trained to deal with this sensitive issue.

Do not frighten the child further by talking about reporting the abuse. In many cases, children who are being abused have been told by their abusers that very bad things will happen to them if they tell anyone. Report the situation immediately to the appropriate authorities and let them handle it.

For information on child abuse, contact:

The National Clearinghouse on Child Abuse and Neglect
330 C Street SW
Washington, DC 20447
Toll-free telephone: 1-800-394-3366
www.calib.com/nccanch

The National Exchange Club Foundation for the Prevention of Child Abuse
3050 Central Avenue
Toledo, OH 43606
Toll-free telephone: 1-800-924-2643
www.preventchildabuse.com

Prevent Child Abuse America
200 South Michigan Avenue, 17th Floor
Chicago, IL 60604
Telephone: (312) 663-3520
www.preventchildabuse.org

25 HEALTHY WAYS TO EXPRESS ANGER

Be careful not to say or do anything to hurt yourself or anyone else.

1. Tell someone you're angry.

2. Talk to yourself in the mirror about your anger.

3. Hit a pillow.

4. Jump up and down.

5. Cry.

6. Hit the floor with a rolled-up newspaper or magazine.

7. Smash play dough or clay.

8. Hit a bed with your fist.

9. Yell "I'M SO ANGRY!!!"

10. Tear and crumple up old newspapers, magazines, or old phone books and fill a garbage bag.

11. Go into a safe room to get some quiet time.

12. Walk away.

13. Lie on a bed with your feet in the air. Kick your feet back and forth and yell "AHHHH!" or "I'M ANGRY!!!"

14. Take a small towel and use it to hit a couch or chair while saying "I'm so angry!"

15. Play an angry song on the piano.

16. Beat a drum.

17. Do an angry dance.

18. Bounce or kick a ball.

19. Dig in the dirt or a sandbox.

20. Have an adult take you swimming; hit the water.

21. Throw rocks into a pond, lake, or ocean.

22. Ask for a hug.

23. Rake leaves or shovel snow.

24. Run.

25. Swing.

LESSON TEN
I Can Choose Not to Hurt Others

Children need to know that it is wrong to hurt others, even when they have been hurt. They need to understand that "getting back" at others only escalates conflict and has other potentially harmful consequences. They need to realize that they always have other choices available to them.

GOALS

1. To teach children that "getting back" at others is not an effective way to resolve conflict.
2. To help children identify the potential consequences of hurtful behavior.
3. To brainstorm positive responses to hurtful actions and remind children that they can choose not to hurt others.

ACTIVITIES

1. The Trouble with "Getting Back"

Remind the children of a recent occasion when two or more of them had a physical altercation of some kind. (You might ask something like, "Who remembers when Abe and Carlos had a fight about the basketball?") Have the participants describe what happened. Afterward, discuss the situation and the outcome. Ask questions like:

- "What was the conflict about?"
- "Who started the (hitting, kicking, pushing, etc.)?"
- "When _____ (the other child) hit (kicked, pushed) back, did that make the conflict better or worse?"
- "Do you think that 'getting back' *ever* makes a conflict better? Or does it *always* make it worse?"

If you can't recall a time when children in your group got into a fight, you can pose a hypothetical example using names of children in your group. ("Let's say that Troy wants to play with a toy that Sarah is using. But Sarah doesn't feel like sharing. So

Troy pushes Sarah, and Sarah pushes back, and Troy hits Sarah, and Sarah hits back. . . .") Recast the questions listed above to fit your hypothetical example.

2. Choices and Consequences

Materials needed:

- Copies of the "Caution" handout on page 35 (best if on bright yellow paper)
- Crayons, colored pencils, and/or markers

Introduce this activity by asking the children, "Who knows what a 'consequence' is?" Guide them to understand a simple definition: *A consequence is something that happens as a result of something else.* Give examples, using the names of children in your group:

- "If Leeza hits Betsy, then Betsy feels hurt. That hurt is a consequence."
- "If Zach pushes Noah down on the playground, Noah might get a bloody knee. His bloody knee is a consequence."
- "If Tracy and Mariah are friends, and Mariah punches Tracy, then Tracy might not want to be friends anymore. Losing a friend is a consequence."
- "If I see Robert push or punch someone else, I'm going to put him on a time-out. The time-out is a consequence."

Give each child a copy of the "Caution" handout. Ask them to think about hurtful things they sometimes feel like doing when they are angry. If they need help getting started, you might refer to the "25 Things That Friends Don't Do" Home Handout from Lesson Three (page 13), or to the list the children brainstormed during that lesson.

Tell the children to use the top half of their handout to draw or write about a hurtful thing they sometimes feel like doing (or a hurtful thing they have actually done). Have them use the bottom half to draw or write about the consequence (potential or real) of that action.

Afterward, ask volunteers to show their finished handouts to the group. Have them tell what they felt like doing (or actually did), and what might have happened (or did happen) as a consequence.

3. What Else Can You Do?

Materials needed:

- Poster paper and easel (or tape the paper to a chalkboard or wall)
- Markers

Ask the children, "If someone hurts you, what else can you do instead of getting back at the person?" Invite the children to brainstorm alternatives. Write down their responses on the poster paper. (If the children have difficulty getting started, give some examples from the "20 Things to Do Instead of Hurting Someone Back" Home Handout on page 36.) Affirm the children's good ideas.

FOLLOW-UP

1. Say to the children, "It's wrong to hurt others, even when they hurt you. In this classroom/group, we do not hurt others. What can we do to help ourselves remember this every day?" Invite suggestions. (*Example:* The children might want to make posters to display in the room.)

2. Tell the children to practice what they have learned today—with their friends, in their group, in their families. Remind them that they now know some positive things to do when people do hurtful things to them. They now know some consequences of doing hurtful things to others. Encourage them to *stop* and *think* before doing anything that might hurt another person. Show an example of the "Stop and Think" Necklace from Lesson Five.

3. Copy the Home Handout for this lesson, "20 Things to Do Instead of Hurting Someone Back," to send home to parents/caregivers. You might use the letter on page 4 to introduce the handout and suggest that parents talk with their child about the items on the list. Point out that these ideas work equally well with siblings!

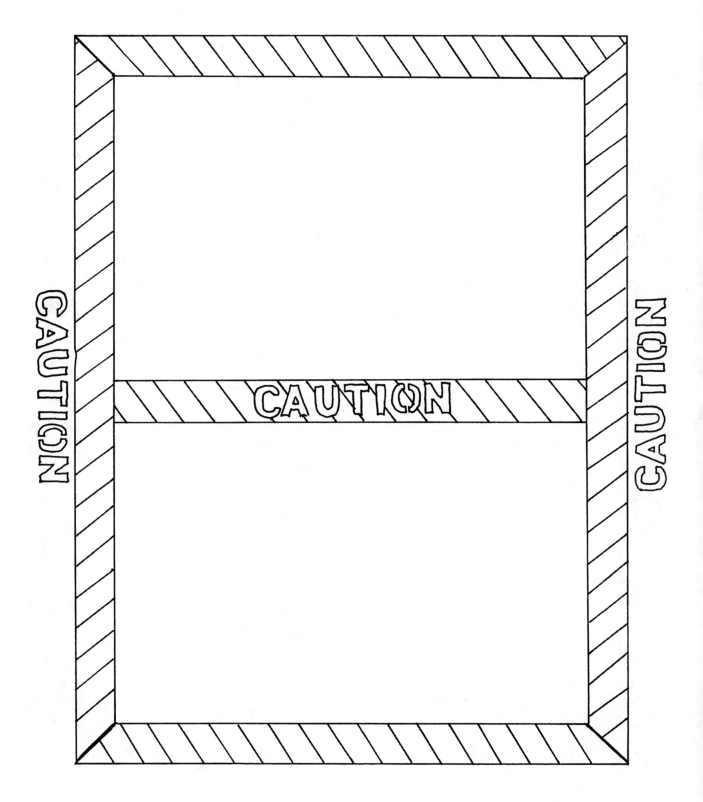

20 THINGS TO DO INSTEAD OF HURTING SOMEONE BACK

When someone hurts you, it's natural to feel angry. Sometimes you might want to get back at the person by hurting him or her. But you can choose not to do that. You can do these things instead:

1. STOP and THINK.

2. Remember that you own your actions. You can decide what to do.

3. Tell yourself, "It's okay to be angry. It's NOT okay to hurt someone else. Even if that person hurt me first."

4. Tell the person, "Stop that! I don't like that!"

5. Keep your hands to yourself. Make fists and put them in your pockets.

6. Keep your feet to yourself. Jump or dance or stomp.

7. Walk away or run away.

8. Tell the person how you feel. Use an "I message." *Example:* "I feel angry when you hit me."

9. Take a deep breath, then blow it out. Blow your angry feelings out of your body.

10. Find an adult. Tell the adult what happened and how you feel.

11. Count slowly from 1 to 10. Count backwards from 10 to 1. Keep counting until you feel your anger getting smaller.

12. Think cool thoughts. Imagine that you're sitting on an iceberg. Cool down your hot, angry feelings.

13. Think happy thoughts. Think of something you like to do. Imagine yourself doing it.

14. Treat the other person with kindness and respect. It won't be easy, but give it a try! This will *totally* surprise the other person, and it might end the conflict then and there.

15. Draw an angry picture.

16. Sing an angry song. Or sing any song EXTRA LOUD.

17. Remember that getting back at someone never makes conflict better. It only makes it worse.

18. Take a time out. Go somewhere until you feel better.

19. Find another person to be with.

20. Know that YOU CAN DO IT. You can choose not to hurt someone else. It's up to you!

LESSON ELEVEN
When Someone Hurts Me. . .

Children need to understand that they don't have to stay in hurtful situations. They can remove themselves physically, they can occupy themselves for a while, and they can ask for help. These are all positive, healthy responses that children need to know about and practice.

GOALS

1. To help children recognize that they have alternatives to remaining in hurtful situations.
2. To encourage children to think of positive, enjoyable things they can do on their own.
3. To help children identify adults they can ask for help in times of need.

ACTIVITIES

1. The "Things That Hurt" Collage

Materials needed:

- Large sheets of paper
- An assortment of magazines with pictures (preferably many pictures of children)
- Crayons, colored pencils, and/or markers
- Glue sticks
- Safety scissors

Ask the children to think about times when friends or other children they know have hurt them—with mean words, hitting, kicking, or in other ways.

You might want to review some examples from the "25 Things That Friends Don't Do" Home Handout from Lesson Three (page 13) or the "Things That Friends Don't Do" list the children brainstormed during that lesson.

Tell the children that they are going to make collages about times when they have been in hurtful situations with their friends or other children they know. They can cut pictures from magazines to illustrate the situations. If they want, they can also write or draw on their collages.

After the children have finished working, invite volunteers to show their collages to the group and tell about the hurtful situation(s) they depict. Ask questions like:

- "What did you do?"
- "Did you stay or leave?"
- "Did you ask for help?"
- *If the child answers yes:* "Who did you ask for help? What happened then?"
- *If the child answers no:* "Was there someone you could have asked for help? Who? Do you think you will ask for help the next time this happens?"

End this activity by saying, "Even when we are in a hurtful situation, we still have choices. We can choose to leave—to get away. We can choose to be alone for a while. And we can choose to ask for help."

NOTE: If you suspect that a child is being abused, see page 31.

2. Things I Can Do by Myself

Materials needed:

- Poster paper and easel (or tape the paper to a chalkboard or wall)
- Markers

Ask the children, "What are your favorite things to do by yourself?" Write down their responses on the poster paper. You might contribute some suggestions from the "50 Things I Can Do by Myself" Home Handout on page 39.

End by saying, "We all know lots of things we can do by ourselves. We can do them when we need to get out of a hurtful situation. Or we can do them when we just want to be alone. It's good to be alone sometimes."

FOLLOW-UP

1. Encourage the children to name one or more adults they can ask for help when they find themselves in hurtful situations. Some children might have already done this in Activity #1; pay special attention now to those children who didn't participate in that discussion. Your goal is to make sure that *every* child can name at least one adult.

2. If your learning environment allows this, invite the children to choose an idea from the "50 Things I Can Do by Myself" Home Handout or the list they brainstormed together, and allow class time for them to pursue their "alone" activities.

3. Copy the Home Handout for this lesson, "50 Things I Can Do by Myself," to send home to parents/caregivers. You might use the letter on page 4 to introduce the handout. Suggest that parents talk with their child about things they (the parents) like to do by themselves. Children need to know that being alone isn't just an alternative to staying in a hurtful situation. It also gives us the chance to pursue our own interests, do things we enjoy, and get to know ourselves better.

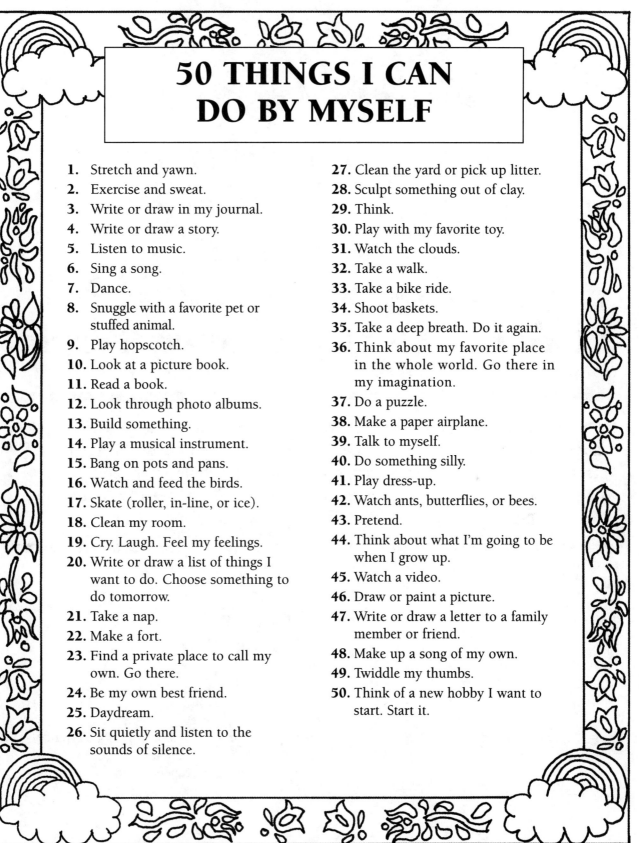

50 THINGS I CAN DO BY MYSELF

1. Stretch and yawn.
2. Exercise and sweat.
3. Write or draw in my journal.
4. Write or draw a story.
5. Listen to music.
6. Sing a song.
7. Dance.
8. Snuggle with a favorite pet or stuffed animal.
9. Play hopscotch.
10. Look at a picture book.
11. Read a book.
12. Look through photo albums.
13. Build something.
14. Play a musical instrument.
15. Bang on pots and pans.
16. Watch and feed the birds.
17. Skate (roller, in-line, or ice).
18. Clean my room.
19. Cry. Laugh. Feel my feelings.
20. Write or draw a list of things I want to do. Choose something to do tomorrow.
21. Take a nap.
22. Make a fort.
23. Find a private place to call my own. Go there.
24. Be my own best friend.
25. Daydream.
26. Sit quietly and listen to the sounds of silence.
27. Clean the yard or pick up litter.
28. Sculpt something out of clay.
29. Think.
30. Play with my favorite toy.
31. Watch the clouds.
32. Take a walk.
33. Take a bike ride.
34. Shoot baskets.
35. Take a deep breath. Do it again.
36. Think about my favorite place in the whole world. Go there in my imagination.
37. Do a puzzle.
38. Make a paper airplane.
39. Talk to myself.
40. Do something silly.
41. Play dress-up.
42. Watch ants, butterflies, or bees.
43. Pretend.
44. Think about what I'm going to be when I grow up.
45. Watch a video.
46. Draw or paint a picture.
47. Write or draw a letter to a family member or friend.
48. Make up a song of my own.
49. Twiddle my thumbs.
50. Think of a new hobby I want to start. Start it.

L E S S O N   T W E L V E
I Can Get Along with Many People

D iversity makes life interesting! When we realize this, and when we seek out and value diversity, we can experience the power of our combined ideas and strengths. Children need to know that all people are inherently valuable, regardless of their differences or similarities. They need to understand that each person is unique, special, and precious.

GOALS

1. To call children's attention to their differences and similarities.
2. To help children appreciate each other's differences.
3. To promote children's openness to accepting people, thoughts, and ideas that are different from their own.

ACTIVITY

People Puzzles

Materials needed:

- Copies of the "People Puzzle" on page 42 (best if copied on heavy paper or light cardboard); for each, cut the pieces apart and put all 4 pieces in an envelope (*tips:* Cut carefully; cut straight through the decorative borders)
- Crayons, colored pencils, and/or markers
- Adhesive tape

Optional:
- Art supplies: Colorful stickers, glitter, bits of ribbon, sequins, etc.
- Glue sticks

Begin by talking with the children about puzzles. Make sure that everyone understands that a puzzle is made up of many pieces of different sizes and shapes, and that when the pieces are put together, they make an interesting whole. Point out that a puzzle isn't complete until all the pieces have been joined together.

Divide the children into groups of four. Give each group an envelope containing the four pieces of a puzzle. Have each child take a puzzle piece and decorate it however he or she chooses. Each child should sign his or her puzzle piece. (Very young children will need help with this.)

NOTE: If the group doesn't divide naturally into fours, decorate the extra puzzle pieces yourself or have some children decorate more than one piece. You should be sure to decorate at least one puzzle piece.

When the children have finished decorating their puzzle pieces, invite them to sit in a circle with their pieces in front of them. Hold up your puzzle piece and say, "I'm looking for a piece that will join with this one." As children say, "Try mine!" you can go around the circle until you find a piece that fits.

Before putting the pieces together, you and the child must each name two ways in which you are different (*examples:* age, hair color, height, clothing, etc.) and two ways in which you are the same (*examples:* both have ten fingers, both are wearing shoes, both have little brothers, both like chocolate, etc.).

Now have the child look for a third piece that joins with the first two. Again, the children must each name two ways in which they are different, and two ways in which they are the same. The child who has the third piece looks for a fourth, and so on until all of the puzzles have been completed—and all of the children know many ways in which

they are different and the same. Encourage the children to go beyond their original foursome when trying to find puzzle pieces that fit.

When all of the puzzles have been completed, use adhesive tape to fasten them together (tape the backs of the puzzles). Arrange the puzzles along a wall or window ledge so everyone can see them all. Talk with the children about how each piece is different. Each is unique—like the children themselves. Yet together, they make interesting and beautiful puzzles. And together, the children make an interesting and beautiful group!

FOLLOW-UP

1. Talk with the children about what they learned from the People Puzzles activity. Ask questions like:

- "Did you learn anything new about each other?"
- "Were you surprised by any ways in which we're different? By any ways in which we're the same?"
- "Do we know each other better now?"

Tell the children, "Each one of us is special and one-of-a-kind. No one is exactly like anyone else. Our differences make us interesting and unique. When we learn about our differences, and when we appreciate and value our differences, this helps us to get along."

2. Copy the Home Handout for this lesson, "Celebrating Diversity," to send home to parents/caregivers. You might use the letter on page 4 to introduce the handout and explain the context ("In this lesson of 'We Can Get Along,' the children learned that they can get along with many people: people who are like them, and people who are not like them.") Suggest that parents talk with their child about appreciating and valuing differences, and the life benefits this yields.

CELEBRATING DIVERSITY

One in four Americans has African, Asian, Hispanic, or Native American ancestry. It's believed that by the year 2050, that number will be one in three. More and more people of color—from South America, India, the Middle East, the Pacific Islands, and other places around the world—are making the United States their home. This increasing diversity is most apparent in the schools.

Your child will likely go through school with people of many different races, as well as varying physical capabilities, skills, talents, learning styles, and needs. In the future, your child will work with all kinds of men and women. You do your child a great service when you promote tolerance and celebrate diversity.

What's in it for your child (and you)?

- If you're tolerant and accepting, you're naturally more open to learning about other people.
- The more you learn, the less you fear.
- The less you fear, the more self-confident and comfortable you feel in all kinds of situations, with all kinds of people.
- You get along better with more people. Because of this, you're likely to be more successful. And your life is definitely more interesting!

The key to getting along with others—and succeeding in today's world—isn't to pretend that differences don't exist. Instead, we need to learn about differences, learn to accept them, and let ourselves enjoy them.

Here are four ways to celebrate diversity with your child:

1. Visit the library together and find books about different cultures, races, abilities, etc. Read them aloud to your child.
2. Seek out opportunities for your child to meet and make friends with a wide variety of children.
3. Make sure that your own circle of friends and acquaintances is diverse, so your child can learn from your example.
4. Talk with your child about ways in which people are different—and the same. Emphasize our common humanity while openly appreciating the characteristics, abilities, and other factors that make us unique.

LESSON THIRTEEN
Friends Are Nice to Be Around

The need to be in relationships with others is one of the most fundamental of all human needs. Children need to know how valuable friendships are, and they need to recognize their own role in creating, strengthening, and maintaining friendships.

GOALS

1. To introduce the idea of friendship as an active, dynamic process of give-and-take.
2. To help children recognize how important their friendships are and how they themselves contribute to these relationships.

ACTIVITY

Friendship Bags

Materials needed:

- Brown paper bags (better if small grocery bags, but you can also use lunch bags)

- An assortment of magazines with pictures (preferably many pictures of children)
- Drawing paper
- Crayons, colored pencils, and/or markers
- Glue sticks
- Safety scissors

Optional:

- Art supplies: Colorful stickers, glitter, bits of ribbon, sequins, etc.

Introduce this lesson by asking each child one or more of these questions:

- "Who are your friends?" (Encourage them to name at least two friends.)
- "Why are those people your friends?" (Guide them to give at least two reasons. *Examples:*

"They are fun to be with; we like to play together; they are nice to me; they understand when I feel sad or angry.")

- "What things do you like to do together?"
- "How do you know they are your friends?"
- "What makes someone a good friend?"

You might want to suggest some of the items from the "25 Qualities of a Good Friend" Home Handout on page 46.

Give each child a paper bag. Explain that the children will use it to make a "Friendship Bag." Have them write their names on their bags. (For very young children, you might want to label the bags before you hand them out.)

Have them cut pictures from magazines that represent their friendships or remind them of their friends. (It will help if you show a few examples: "Look, here's a picture of two people laughing together. Does this remind you of anything?" "Here's a picture of people riding bikes together. They seem to be having a lot of fun. Do you ride bikes with your friends?" "Here is a picture of two people sitting together on a bench. It looks like they are sharing some quiet time together. Have you ever shared quiet time with a friend?") When the children have found and cut out the pictures they want to use, have them glue their pictures to the *outside* of their bags.

Shift the children's focus by asking:

- "Why are these people friends with you? What do *you* do to be a friend?"
- "What makes *you* a good friend?"

Refer again to the "25 Qualities of a Good Friend" Home Handout on page 46. Ask the children if they have these qualities.

Now ask the children to draw a picture that shows them being a good friend. Encourage them to think about this before they start drawing. What qualities of being a good friend do they want to show? When they are finished drawing, have them put their pictures *inside* of their bags.

Invite the children to bring their bags and sit in a circle. Give each child the opportunity to tell about his or her friendships. You might ask questions like:

- "Why did you choose those particular pictures to glue on the outside of your bag?"
- "Tell us what's happening in the picture that shows _____."
- "What do you think these pictures say about your friendships?" (*Examples:* We like to laugh; we like to play together; we enjoy playing sports; we like to go shopping.)

Next, have the child open the bag and share the picture of himself or herself. Ask questions like:

- "How does this show you being a good friend?"
- "What do you like most about this picture?"

End the activity by saying something like, "It seems as if we all have good friends. And we all *are* good friends. Every friendship is a work of art—just like the 'Friendship Bag' you made today."

FOLLOW-UP

1. Talk with the children about how we don't exist in this world alone. Friendships are essential to rich and happy lives. They help us learn about the world—and ourselves. Good friendships bring out the best in us.

2. Help the children to recognize that each of them has a lot to offer a friendship, and that it takes two to make a friendship work.

3. Copy the Home Handout for this lesson, "25 Qualities of a Good Friend," to send home to parents/caregivers. You might use the letter on page 4 to introduce the handout and encourage parents to talk with their child about the importance of friendship.

25 QUALITIES OF A GOOD FRIEND

A good friend is:

1. Kind.

2. Respectful.

3. Understanding.

4. Helpful.

5. Someone who doesn't judge me.

6. Honest.

7. A good listener.

8. Someone who is around when I need him or her.

9. Playful.

10. Fun to be with.

11. Trustworthy.

12. Supportive.

13. Encouraging.

14. Giving.

15. Someone who knows what I'm feeling.

16. Willing to work with me.

17. Someone who has a good sense of humor.

18. Thoughtful.

19. Someone I can talk to.

20. Patient.

21. Tolerant.

22. Comfortable to be around.

23. Loyal.

24. Loving.

25. A wonderful and important part of my life.

LESSON FOURTEEN
No Two People Are the Same

Every child is a unique individual, with his or her own wants, needs, thoughts, and feelings. Children need to know that it isn't necessary for everyone to always agree with each other—not even friends. They also need to know that when they disagree, they can do so without anger or hurtful words or behaviors. Children need to learn that they may sometimes have to "agree to disagree" in order to blend individuals in relationships that work.

GOALS

1. To help children recognize that even friends don't always agree with each other.
2. To introduce the concept of "agreeing to disagree."
3. To give children practice in agreeing to disagree.

ACTIVITIES

1. The Anger Tornado

Materials needed:

- A copy of the "Anger Tornado" on page 50 (best if copied on medium-weight to heavy paper), cut out along the lines (start at the X and cut around the spiral)

Optional:

- Copies of the "Anger Tornado" on page 50 for the children OR drawing paper, crayons,

colored pencils, paints, and/or markers so they can make their own
- Safety scissors

Ask the children, "Is there anyone who's right about everything, all of the time? Is there anyone who's *never* wrong? Anyone who's 100 percent perfect?" The children will probably say no.

Say, "Sometimes we act as if we're right all the time. This can cause problems. It can make conflict worse. It can cause an Anger Tornado."

Very slowly lift the cut-out "Anger Tornado" by the X as you explain this with an example like the following, using the names of children in your group:

"Let's say that Ben and Tara don't agree about something. Maybe Ben likes popcorn and Tara doesn't. One day, Ben says, 'I really like popcorn,' and Tara says, 'Popcorn is gross.' So Ben says, 'If you think popcorn is gross, you're stupid!' Ben is really angry at Tara for disagreeing with him.

"Tara doesn't understand why Ben is so angry. So she thinks something like this: 'If Ben is angry at me, I must have done something wrong. If I've done something wrong, I must be bad. But I don't want to be bad! So I have to fight with Ben about his right to be angry.' She says to Ben, 'I think YOU'RE stupid!' And the conflict between them gets worse."

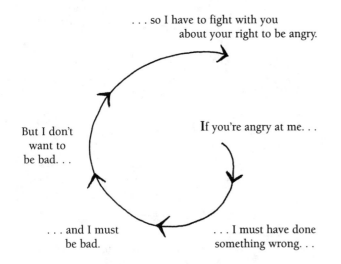

. . . so I have to fight with you about your right to be angry.

But I don't want to be bad. . .

If you're angry at me. . .

. . . and I must be bad.

. . . I must have done something wrong. . .

By now, you should be holding up the tornado in front of the children. Slowly lower it as you say, "But Tara has another choice. She can agree to disagree with Ben. She can say, 'I guess you like popcorn and I don't. That's okay. We don't always have to like the same things.'" Continue lowering the tornado until it lays flat.

If time allows, hand out copies of the "Anger Tornado" and let children decorate them and cut them out. Or hand out drawing paper and let them draw and decorate their own anger tornadoes. You might hang them around the room for the remainder of this lesson.

2. Agreeing to Disagree

Say, "Guess what? People don't always have to agree on everything! Even friends don't have to agree on everything. People can agree to disagree. When this happens, no one feels 'wrong' or 'bad.' And no one has to fight or argue. Agreeing to disagree is a great way to reduce or avoid conflict."

Invite volunteers to role play situations in which they agree to disagree. You might use situations like the following or invent your own, based on real examples from the children's experience. The situations should lead to conclusions like those given here:

- Ben and Tina are watching a movie together. Ben thinks the movie is funny; Tina thinks it's boring. (There can be more than one way to view the same thing. People have different likes and dislikes, feelings and opinions.)
- Su Li loaned Amos one of her favorite drawings a long time ago, and now she wants it back. But Amos says that he already gave it back. Su Li can't find it, and Amos doesn't have it. The drawing seems to be lost. (Some problems don't have solutions.)
- Erik is bragging about his new bike to Tony. Erik thinks that his bike is better than Tony's. But Tony thinks that his bike is better than Erik's. (Sometimes there is no "right" or "wrong" answer to a problem.)

- Juanita and Stephan are best friends who both love baseball. But Juanita likes the Yankees, and Stephan likes the Braves. They spend a lot of time talking about which team is best and why. (It's okay to disagree with someone and still value that person as a friend.)

End by saying that if everyone always agreed with everyone else, the world would be a boring place. We can all learn from people whose opinions and ideas are different from ours.

FOLLOW-UP

Tell the children to practice what they learned today—with their friends, in the group, in their families. Remind them that agreeing to disagree is a good way to avoid conflict.

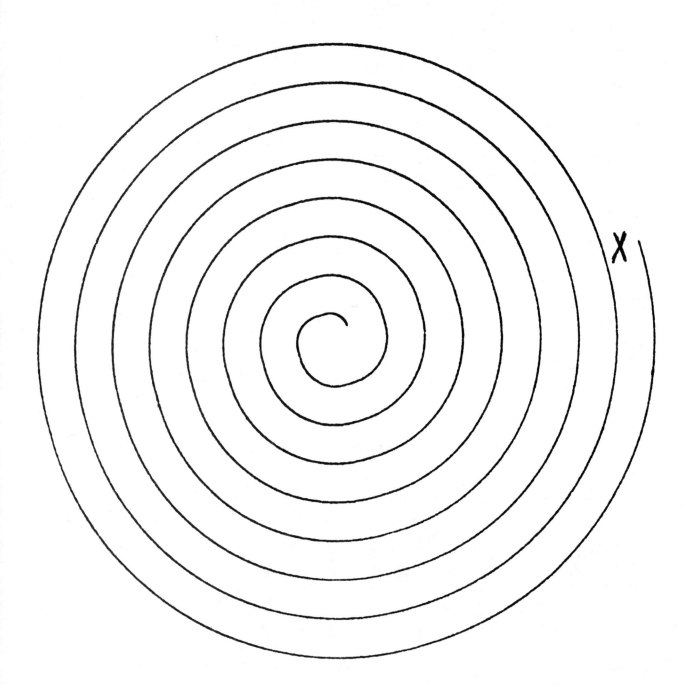

LESSON FIFTEEN
We Can Get Along

Learning to get along and resolve conflicts is a lifelong process. If children can learn how to deal effectively with conflicts and build healthy relationships, they will have the tools they need to establish rich and rewarding connections with others throughout their lives.

GOALS

1. To review and reinforce the skills and concepts presented throughout "We Can Get Along."
2. To celebrate what children have learned and encourage them to keep practicing their new skills.

ACTIVITIES

1. The "We Can Get Along" Rainbow Banner

Materials needed:

- Blank newsprint, butcher paper, poster paper, or other large sheets of paper for making a group banner
- Crayons, colored pencils, and/or markers
- Paints
- Art supplies: Glitter, confetti, bits of ribbon, colorful stickers, etc.
- An assortment of magazines with pictures

- Glue sticks
- Safety scissors

Introduce the idea that getting along with others is like living under a rainbow. Work with the children to paint a large rainbow banner. Along the way, explain that the different colors of the rainbow stand for skills they have learned in "We Can Get Along":

Red = We are responsible for our own words and actions.
Orange = We can stop and think before we speak and act.
Yellow = We can cooperate and negotiate.
Green = We can treat others the way we like to be treated.
Blue = We can appreciate each other's differences.
Indigo = We can be good friends to other people.
Violet = We can agree to disagree.

Write these statements in the colors of the rainbow, and title the banner "We Can Get Along." Or, if you prefer, you can title the banner "How to Get Along" and use these shorter versions of the statements:

Red = Be Responsible.
Orange = Stop and Think.
Yellow = Cooperate and Negotiate.
Green = Treat Others Kindly.
Blue = Appreciate Differences.
Indigo = Be a Friend.
Violet = Agree to Disagree.

Invite the children to decorate the banner—with pictures cut from magazines of people getting along, glued around and under the rainbow; and with other decorations they choose. Obviously, this should be a cooperative project from beginning to end!

You might want to see if you can display the finished banner in a public place—perhaps in the hallway or a community center.

2. Individual "We Can Get Along" Rainbow Pictures

Materials needed:

- Drawing paper
- Crayons, colored pencils, and/or markers

Have the children create individual "getting along" rainbows. Under the rainbow, they can draw a scene from their own life—a time when they got along with a friend, classmate, or family member. When the children are finished, gather them into a circle and invite them to talk about their pictures.

FOLLOW-UP

1. Ask if the children have any questions about what they have learned during "We Can Get Along." You might also ask:

- "What are the skills you've learned for resolving conflicts?"
- "How will these skills help you in the future?"
- "Do you think you will do better now at getting along with others? Why?"
- "What was your favorite part of 'We Can Get Along'?"

2. Congratulate the children for completing the course. Give each child a copy of the "I Can Get Along" handout to take home, decorate, share with their parents, and hang on a wall or bedroom door. Thank them for being so enjoyable and for working so hard.

3. Copy the Home Handout for this lesson, "20 Tips for Getting Along," to send home to parents/caregivers. You might use the letter on page 4 to introduce the handout and explain that it summarizes the concepts and skills the children learned during "We Can Get Along." Encourage parents to talk with their child about the tips. Suggest that they praise and congratulate their child for completing the course.

I CAN GET ALONG

My name is

_____.

I can be responsible for my words and actions.

I can *stop* and *think* before I speak or act.

I can cooperate and negotiate.

I can treat others the way I like to be treated.

I can appreciate differences.

I can be a good friend.

I can agree to disagree.

I can make good choices.

I can keep my hands to myself.

I can help to resolve conflicts.

I can get along with others!

20 TIPS FOR GETTING ALONG

1. Understand that conflict is a normal part of life.

2. Be honest about your feelings, wants, and needs. Use "I messages" and avoid "you messages," which blame the other person and put him or her on the defensive. *Examples:* Try "I don't like it when you take my things without asking" instead of "You always take my things without asking."

3. Build a feelings vocabulary so you can say what you mean.

4. Be responsible for your own words and actions.

5. Use your own feelings as a guide when choosing your words and actions. Try your best to make good choices.

6. *Stop* and *think* before you speak or act.

7. Try to see a conflict from the other person's point of view. Instead of thinking, "How can *I* get what *I* want?" try thinking, "How can we *both* get what we need?"

8. Be willing to negotiate and compromise.

9. Treat other people with kindness and respect—the way you like to be treated.

10. Don't use mean and hurtful words.

11. Don't hit. Hitting is never okay. (The same goes for pushing, punching, scratching, biting, kicking, pinching, and other hurtful actions.)

12. Know that your words and actions have consequences. *Stop* and *think* about the consequences ahead of time.

13. If you feel angry, express your anger in healthy ways. It's okay to feel angry; it's *not* okay to take out your anger on other people.

14. Don't get back at others. Getting back never makes a conflict better. It always makes it worse.

15. If you are in a hurtful situation, get away as soon as you can. Be alone for a while and do something you enjoy.

16. If you are in a hurtful situation, get help.

17. Understand that *all* people are valuable and each person is unique.

18. Appreciate differences. They make life interesting!

19. Be a good friend.

20. If you try and try but still can't resolve your conflict, agree to disagree.

Recommended Reading

BOOKS FOR CHILDREN

Berenstain, Stan, and Jan Berenstain. *The Berenstain Bears and the Bully* (Random House, 1993). When confronted by a bully, Sister Bear learns a valuable lesson in self-defense and forgiveness. Ages 3–6.

Durell, Ann, and Marilyn Sachs, editors. *The Big Book for Peace* (Dutton, 1990). A collection of stories, pictures, poems, and songs—all promoting the cause of peace—from over 30 well-known illustrators and children's authors. Ages 7–12.

The Editors of Conari Press. *Kids' Random Acts of Kindness* (Conari Press, 1994). Kids from around the world tell their own stories of sudden, impetuous acts of kindness—times when they reached out to a stranger, helped out at home, or gave of themselves in other ways. All ages.

Lalli, Judy. *Make Someone Smile and 40 More Ways to Be a Peaceful Person* (Free Spirit Publishing Inc., 1996). In simple words and appealing black-and-white photographs, children model the skills of peacemaking and conflict resolution. All ages.

Leaf, Munro. *The Story of Ferdinand* (Viking, 1936). The early childhood classic about a young bull who would rather smell the flowers than fight. Ages 3–8.

Lobel, Arnold. *Frog and Toad Are Friends* (Harper & Row, 1970). Heads of state could learn much about strategies for conflict resolution and harmonious relationships from this easy reader. Ages 5–8.

Naylor, Phyllis Reynolds. *King of the Playground* (Atheneum, 1991). A young boy's father helps him develop creative strategies for dealing with the playground bully. Ages 3–8.

Olofsdotter, Marie. *Frej the Fearless* (*The Secret World of Frej*) (Free Spirit Publishing Inc., 1993). Frej saves Queen Feather-Duster from the Hairy Beast by discovering that love is stronger than the sword. Ages 5 and up.

Scholes, Katherine. *Peace Begins with You* (Little, Brown, 1990). Explains in simple terms the concept of peace, why conflict occurs, how to resolve conflicts in positive ways, and how to protect peace. Ages 6–11.

Seuss, Dr. *The Butter Battle Book* (Random House, 1984). A conflict arises when two towns argue over whether bread should be eaten butter-side-up or butter-side-down. In this great discussion starter, the reader is left to decide how the story should end. Ages 5 and up.

Surat, Michele Maria. *Angel Child, Dragon Child* (Steck-Vaughn Company, 1992). A Vietnamese girl is taunted by an American boy, and the two get into a playground fight—but something wonderful happens when they try to understand each other and get along. Ages 5–8.

Zolotow, Charlotte. *The Quarreling Book* (Harper, 1963). A quarrel spreads from one person to another in an epidemic of bad feelings, but the process is reversed when the family dog refuses to reciprocate. Ages 3–8.

BOOKS FOR ADULTS

Cecil, Nancy Lee, with Patricia L. Roberts. *Raising Peaceful Children in a Violent World* (LuraMedia Books, 1995). Offers creative and practical ways to teach children peaceful conflict resolution. Includes chapters on family communication, conflict resolution, discipline strategies, racial attitudes, gender stereotypes, TV, toys, games, and books. For use with children of all ages.

Crary, Elizabeth. *Kids Can Cooperate: A Practical Guide to Teaching Problem Solving* (Parenting Press, 1984). Describes how to motivate and teach children the skills they need to resolve conflicts by themselves. For teachers and parents of toddlers to kindergartners.

Delisle, Deb, and Jim Delisle. *Growing Good Kids: 28 Activities to Enhance Self-Awareness, Compassion, and Leadership* (Free Spirit Publishing Inc., 1996). Created by teachers and classroom-tested, these activities build skills in problem solving, decision making, cooperative learning, divergent thinking, communication, and more, while promoting healthy self-awareness, tolerance, character development, and service to others. For teachers of grades 3–8.

Drew, Naomi. *Learning the Skills of Peacemaking: A K–6 Activity Guide on Resolving Conflict, Communicating, Cooperating* (Jalmar Press, 1995). This guide helps teachers and parents bring the skills of peacemaking to real-life situations and integrate conflict resolution into all subject areas. Activities teach self-awareness, sensitivity to others, interconnectedness, and more. For teachers and parents of ages 5–12.

Frankel, Fred. *Good Friends Are Hard to Find: Help Your Child Find, Make and Keep Friends* (Perspective Publishing, 1996). Step by step, parents learn how to help their children make friends, solve problems with other kids, and deal with teasing, bullying, and meanness. For parents of ages 5–12.

Janke, Rebecca, and Julie Peterson. *The Peacemaker's A,B,Cs for Young Children: A Guide for Teaching Conflict Resolution with a Peace Table* (Growing Communities for Peace, 1995). A step-by-step manual crammed with ways to create a peacemaking environment, focus on the positive, and become a role model for children. For use with ages 3–9.

Levin, Diane E. *Teaching Young Children in Violent Times: Building a Peaceable Classroom* (Kendall/Hunt Publishing Co., 1996). Offers guidelines and activities to help children resolve conflict, appreciate diversity, meet safety needs, and find alternatives to violent behavior.

Mathias, Barbara, and Mary Ann French. *40 Ways to Raise a Nonracist Child* (HarperCollins, 1996). Provides families with the tools they need to talk openly about racism and to respect and appreciate racial differences. For parents, educators, counselors, and caregivers of children from toddler to teenager.

Rice, Judith Anne. *The Kindness Curriculum: Introducing Young Children to Loving Values* (Redleaf Press, 1995). Activities help to instill character and create opportunities for kids to practice kindness, empathy, conflict resolution, and respect.

Smith, Charles A. *The Peaceful Classroom: 162 Easy Activities to Teach Preschoolers Compassion and Cooperation* (Gryphon House, Inc., 1993). Use this resource to plan time devoted to developing the skills of cooperation, friendship, compassion, and kindness. Activities are organized by age and skill. For teachers of preschool and kindergarten.

Whitham, Cynthia. *Win the Whining War & Other Skirmishes: A Family Peace Plan* (Perspective Publishing, 1991). Increase cooperation and reduce conflict quickly with these easy-to-use techniques from the renowned UCLA Parent Training Program. For parents of ages 2–12.

About the Authors

Lauren Murphy Payne, M.S.W., is a psychotherapist in private practice at the White-Leonard Clinic in Racine, Wisconsin. She has appeared on metropolitan Milwaukee television talk shows and is a frequent speaker at local, regional, state, and national conferences. She authored and appeared in the video series, "Making Anger Work for You," produced and distributed by Greystone Educational Materials. Ms. Murphy Payne lives in Racine and has two school-aged children.

Claudia Rohling, M.S.W., is an artist, illustrator, and art therapist whose work is sold throughout the United States and Canadian international gift markets. Her work has been featured on the covers of *Leisure Arts: The Magazine* and *Celebrations* and on materials produced by The National Committee to Prevent Child Abuse. Claudia is the owner of Rohling Studios, where she oversees production, distribution, and creative development of her work as prints and greeting cards; an art therapist at Charter Hospital in West Allis, Wisconsin; and cofounder and creative director of The Turning Point speaking and consulting service, which offers training, workshops, and seminars on a variety of topics. She has been a speaker for local, regional, state, and national conferences. She lives in Racine, Wisconsin, and is the mother of three young adults.

Also by Lauren Murphy Payne and Claudia Rohling:

- *We Can Get Along: A Child's Book of Choices*
- *Just Because I Am: A Child's Book of Affirmation*
- *A Leader's Guide to Just Because I Am*

Other Great Books from Free Spirit

We Can Get Along
A Child's Book of Choices
by Lauren Murphy Payne, M.S.W., illustrated by Claudia Rohling, M.S.W.
Simple words and inviting illustrations teach children how to get along with others and resolve conflicts peacefully. For ages 3–8.
$9.95; 36 pp.; softcover; color illus.; 7⅝" x 9¼"

Leader's Guide
by Lauren Murphy Payne, M.S.W., and Claudia Rohling, M.S.W.
For preschool through grade 3.
$14.95; 64 pp.; softcover; illus., 8½" x 11"

"Written with clarity, authority, and empathy . . . lively and appealing . . . the Golden Rule in sensible, easily understood language."
—*School Library Journal*

Just Because I Am
A Child's Book of Affirmation
by Lauren Murphy Payne, M.S.W., illustrated by Claudia Rohling, M.S.W.
Warm, simple words and enchanting full-color illustrations strengthen and support children's self-esteem. Ideal for early elementary, preschool, day care, and the home. For ages 3–8.
$9.95; 32 pp.; softcover; color illus.; 7⅝" x 9¼"

Leader's Guide
by Lauren Murphy Payne, M.S.W., and Claudia Rohling, M.S.W.
For preschool through grade 3.
$14.95; 56 pp.; softcover; illus., 8½" x 11"

"Simple but empowering . . . teaches children ages 3 to 8 to trust their bodies, that all of their feelings are OK and that they have the power to say 'No' to anything that feels dangerous or wrong."
—*Chicago Tribune*

I'm Like You, You're Like Me
A Child's Book About Understanding and Celebrating Each Other
by Cindy Gainer
"You and I are alike in many ways. We may be the same age or live on the same street. . . . We are different from each other, too." Simple words and lush illustrations draw children into this gentle story of discovery, acceptance, and affirmation. For ages 3–8.
$12.95; 48 pp.; softcover; color illus.; 11¼" x 9"

Leader's Guide
by Cindy Gainer
For preschool through grade 3.
$16.95; 80 pp.; softcover; illus., 8½" x 11"

"Understanding diversity cannot start too early. This simple, colorful picture book introduces children to the concept of respecting others. The basics of friendship . . . are all explained with illustrations that make the reader smile."
—Parent Council®

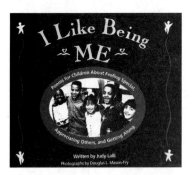

I Like Being Me
Poems for Children About Feeling Special, Appreciating Others, and Getting Along
by Judy Lalli, M.S., photographs by Douglas L. Mason-Fry
Rhyming poems and black and white photographs explore issues important to young children—being kind, solving problems, and more. For ages 3–8.
$9.95; 64 pp.; softcover; B&W photos; 8¼" x 7¼"

"Veteran teacher Judy Lalli is right on the mark. These poems communicate with a genuineness that children will appreciate."
—*Family Life*

Make Someone Smile and 40 More Ways to Be a Peaceful Person
by Judy Lalli, M.S., photographs by Douglas L. Mason-Fry
Simple words and warm, appealing black-and-white photographs present clear and understandable ideas for being a peaceful person and promoting peaceful thoughts and behaviors. The photographs feature children of many races modeling the skills of peacemaking and conflict resolution in their everyday lives. For all ages.
$9.95; 80 pp.; softcover; B&W photos; 8¼" x 7¼"

"Even the pictures make you smile and feel that the next generation is on the way to a better world."
—*American Bookseller*, "Booksellers Pick the Best"

"The simple format has a strong, clear impact."
—*Green Teacher*

Hands Are Not for Hitting
by Martine Agassi, Ph.D.
In this gentle, encouraging book, psychologist Martine Agassi helps young children understand that they are capable of positive, loving actions. Simple words and warm, inviting full-color illustrations reinforce the underlying concepts: that violence is never okay, and kids can learn to manage their anger. Made to be read aloud, this book also includes a special section for adults, with ideas for things to talk about and activities to do together. For ages 2–6.
$11.95; 40 pp.; softcover; color illus.; 9" x 9"

Hands Are Not for Hitting Board Book
by Martine Agassi, Ph.D., illustrated by Marieka Heinlen
This version of *Hands* is shorter and simpler. There are fewer pages and fewer words. The print is bigger, and so are the full-color illustrations. Because it's a board book, it's virtually indestructible, making it a great first book for toddlers. Bright, inviting, accessible, and durable, this book belongs everywhere young children are. For ages 1½–3.
$7.95; 24 pp.; hardcover; color illus.; 7" x 7"

Hands Are Not for Hitting Poster
$9.95; printed on heavy stock; 18" x 24"

To place an order or to request a free catalog of SELF-HELP FOR KIDS® and SELF-HELP FOR TEENS® materials, please write, call, email, or visit our Web site:

Free Spirit Publishing Inc.
217 Fifth Avenue North • Suite 200 • Minneapolis, MN 55401-1299
toll-free 800.735.7323 • local 612.338.2068 • fax 612.337.5050
help4kids@freespirit.com • www.freespirit.com

Visit us on the Web!
www.freespirit.com

Stop by anytime to find our Parents' Choice Approved catalog with fast, easy, secure 24-hour online ordering; "Ask Our Authors," where visitors ask questions—and authors give answers—on topics important to children, teens, parents, teachers, and others who care about kids; links to other Web sites we know and recommend; fun stuff for everyone, including quick tips and strategies from our books; and much more! Plus our site is completely searchable so you can find what you need in a hurry. Stop in and let us know what you think!

Just point and click!

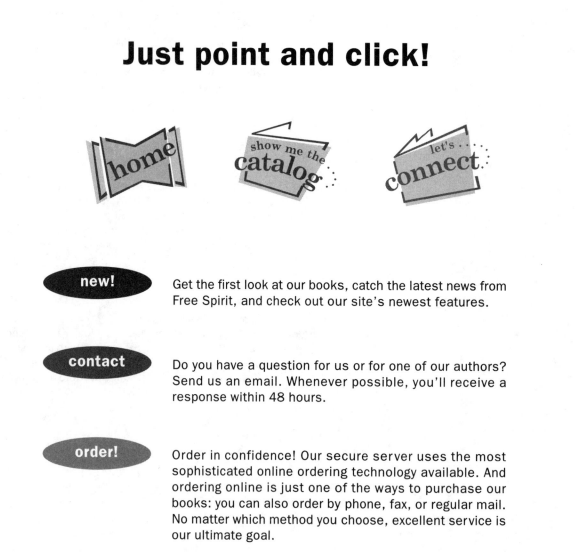

new! Get the first look at our books, catch the latest news from Free Spirit, and check out our site's newest features.

contact Do you have a question for us or for one of our authors? Send us an email. Whenever possible, you'll receive a response within 48 hours.

order! Order in confidence! Our secure server uses the most sophisticated online ordering technology available. And ordering online is just one of the ways to purchase our books: you can also order by phone, fax, or regular mail. No matter which method you choose, excellent service is our ultimate goal.

1.800.735.7323 • fax 612.337.5050 • help4kids@freespirit.com